Around the World

Transportation

Margaret C. Hall

Heinemann Library
Chicago, Illinois

Designed by Lisa Buckley
Printed in China

06
10 9 8 7 6 5 4 3

Library of Congress Cataloging-in-Publication Data
Hall, Margaret, 1947-
    Transportation / Margaret C. Hall.
        p. cm. -- (Around the world)
    Includes bibliographical references and index.
    ISBN 1-58810-104-5 (library binding) (HC), 1-4034-4007-7 (Pbk.)
    ISBN 978-1-58810-104-4 (library binding) (HC), 978-1-4034-4007-5 (Pbk.)
        1. Transportation--Juvenile literature. [1. Transportation.] I. Title. II. Around the world
(Chicago, Ill.)

TA1149 .H345 2001   388--dc21
                                                                00-063272

Acknowledgments
The author and publishers are grateful to the following for permission to reproduce copyright material:
Oliver Benn/Tony Stone, pp. 1, 20; Wolfgang Kaehler, pp., 4a; Keren Su/Tony Stone, p. 4b; Sharon Smith/Bruce Coleman, Inc., p. 4c; Tony Freeman/Photo Edit, pp., 5, 13; Glen Allison/Tony Stone, p. 6; Robert Van Der Hilst/Tony Stone, p. 7; Art Wolfe/Tony Stone, p. 8; David Young-Wolff/Photo Edit, p. 9; Keith Wood/Tony Stone, p.10; J.C. Carton/Bruce Coleman, Inc., p. 11; D. MacDonald/Photo Edit, p. 12; Rudi Von Briel/Photo Edit, p. 14; Bill Bachmann/Photo Edit, pp. 15, 19; Joe McDonald/Bruce Coleman, Inc., p. 16; F. Greenberg/Photo Edit, p. 17; Paul Conklin/Photo Edit, p. 18; Bob Stovall/Bruce Coleman, Inc., p. 21; Robert Brenner/Photo Edit, p. 22; Kent Foster/Bruce Coleman, Inc., p. 23; Kenneth Jarecke/The Stock Market, p. 24; Anna E. Zuckermann/Photo Edit, p. 25; David Madison/Bruce Coleman, Inc., p. 26; Kim Saar/Heinemann Library, p. 27; Andy Sacks/Tony Stone, p. 28; R. Rainey/Photo Edit, p. 29.

Cover: Robert Van Der Hilst/Tony Stone

Every effort has been made to contact copyright holders of any material reproduced in this book. Any omissions will be rectified in subsequent printings if notice is given to the publisher.

Some words are shown in bold, **like this.** You can find out what they mean by looking in the glossary.

Contents

People Have Needs .4

Why People Travel .6

Transportation Around the World 8

Transporting Goods 10

Transportation Long Ago and Today 12

Travel by Foot 14

Travel by Animal .16

Travel by Water 18

Travel by Road 20

Travel by Rail 22

Travel by Air 24

Moving Large Groups of People 26

In the Future 28

Amazing Transportation Facts 30

Glossary 31

More Books to Read 32

Index 32

People Have Needs

People everywhere have the same **needs**. They need food, clothing, water, and homes. They also need to be able to get from place to place.

Where people live makes a difference in what they eat and wear. It makes a difference in their homes and the kinds of **transportation** they use.

Why People Travel

People travel for many reasons. They go to work and school. They go places to buy or gather things they need.

People also travel for fun. They visit family and friends who live in other cities or countries. Some people travel just to see new places.

Transportation Around the World

Transportation is what moves people or **goods** from place to place. The kind of transportation people use depends on the **resources** they have close by.

Some kinds of transportation carry only a few people at a time. Others can move large numbers of people.

Transporting Goods

Many people use **goods** that are not found where they live. These goods must be moved from where they are made or grown.

How goods are moved depends on what they are. It also depends on their **value** and how far they have to travel.

Transportation Long Ago and Today

Transportation is always changing. Long ago, people walked or rode on animals. They still do. But today people also travel in faster ways.

Transportation **inventions** have made travel easier and faster. Riding a bicycle is faster than walking. Traveling by car or another **motor vehicle** is even faster.

Travel by Foot

Walking is the oldest form of **transportation**. It is still common in many places. Even people who own cars often walk for short distances.

In some places, people use their feet to move **passengers**. They run or pedal bicycles to pull carts or small carriages.

Travel by Animal

In many places, animals are used for **transportation**. People ride horses, oxen, camels, and even elephants. Sometimes the animals pull carts or wagons with **passengers** inside.

Pack animals are used to move **goods** from place to place. The animals carry packages, bundles, and even large boxes on their backs.

Travel by Water

In some places, there are few roads, or the roads are very crowded. It is easier to travel on rivers, lakes, and **canals**.

Many kinds of boats are used to move people, cars, and other **goods**. Some boats go short distances. Others can travel all the way across an ocean.

Travel by Road

Some kinds of **transportation** need roads.
Many roads are not much more than
dirt or **gravel** paths. Others are wide with
smooth surfaces that make it easy to
travel quickly.

Bicycles, cars, buses, and trucks travel on roads. Some areas have miles and miles of good roads. People in those places usually travel by **motor vehicle.**

Travel by Rail

Trains, **subways**, and **streetcars** all move along on **rails** or tracks. Rail travel is important in large cities. People can travel faster by subway than they can on crowded streets.

Trains are very important in places where there are few good roads. Some rail **systems** cover short distances. Others go across many different countries.

Travel by Air

Airplanes are used to travel long distances quickly. **Commercial** airplanes carry hundreds of people. **Private** airplanes are usually smaller and carry only a few people.

Sometimes the only way to get somewhere is by airplane. In places where there are not many roads, small planes can land in a field. A seaplane can even land on water.

Moving Large Groups of People

In large cities, many people travel at the same time. Special kinds of **transportation** are used, such as buses, **subways**, and **commuter** trains.

In most cities, people travel in **motor vehicles**. But people do not always use cars. Some cities have commuter boats!

In the Future

Transportation scientists and **inventors** are always at work. They are thinking about ways to make travel faster, easier, and safer.

Soon, more people might drive electric cars. Trains might move at very high speeds. Whatever happens, all over the world people will still be moving from place to place.

Amazing Transportation Facts

✪ Some forms of **transportation** can move in more than one way. **Amphibious vehicles** are like boats on wheels. They can travel on land and then drive into the water.

✪ Japan's bullet train gets its name from its bullet-like shape and its speed. A bullet train travels three times faster than most cars do.

✪ There are now trains called maglevs that move without **rails**. They get their power from magnets.

✪ Space shuttles are a form of transportation. Someday people may use shuttles to take trips to the moon or a space station!

Glossary

amphibious vehicle   something that can go on land and water

canal   human-made waterway

commercial   airline that flies anyone who buys a ticket to different places

commuter   way of travel that goes short distances, usually from peoples' homes to their jobs and back

goods   things that will be sold to people

gravel   small stone

invention   useful object that no one has thought of before

inventor   someone who creates new ideas and objects

motor vehicle   any form of road transportation that uses a motor to move

needs   things people must have in order to live

pack animal   animal, such as a donkey or camel, that is used to carry things

passenger   traveler who rides or is carried to where he or she is going

private   owned and used by one person or company

rail   track on which vehicles travel

resource   item available for use

streetcar   bus-like vehicle that travels on tracks set into a street

subway   underground train

system   group of things that work together

transportation   ways people move from place to place

value   how much something is worth

More Books to Read

Oxlade, Chris. *Bicycles*. Chicago: Heinemann Library, 2000.

—. *Boats and Ships*. Chicago: Heinemann Library, 2000.

Saunders-Smith, Gail. *Airplanes*. Danbury, Conn.: Children's Press, 1998.

—. *Cars*. Danbury, Conn.: Children's Press, 1998.

Index

air travel 24–25
airplane 24–25
amphibious vehicle 30
bicycle 13, 15, 21
boat 19, 27, 30
bus 21, 26
canal 18
car 13, 14, 21, 27, 29
carriage 15
foot travel 14–15

goods 8, 10–11, 17, 19
invention 13, 28
inventor 28
maglev 30
motor vehicle 13, 21, 27
needs 4, 6
pack animals 17
rail travel 22–23, 26, 30
road 18, 20–21

seaplane 25
space shuttle 30
streetcar 22
subway 22, 26
train 22, 23, 29, 30
commuter 26
travel by animal 12, 16–17
truck 21
walking 12–13, 14–15
water travel 18–19